THE CHRONICLES OF NARNIA

OFFICIAL COLORING BOOK

FEATURING ORIGINAL ARTWORK
BY PAULINE BAYNES
FROM ALL SEVEN BOOKS

THE MAGICIAN'S
NEPHEW

NO GREAT WISDOM

—Uncle Andrew

THE MAGICIAN'S NEPHEW

CAN BE REACHED WITHOUT SACRIFICE.

First came the hansom. There was no one in the driver's seat. On the roof—not sitting, but standing on the roof —swaying with superb balance as it came at full speed round the corner with one wheel in the air—was Jadis the Queen of Queens and the Terror of Charn.

Out of the trees wild people stepped forth, gods and Fauns and Satyrs and Dwarfs.

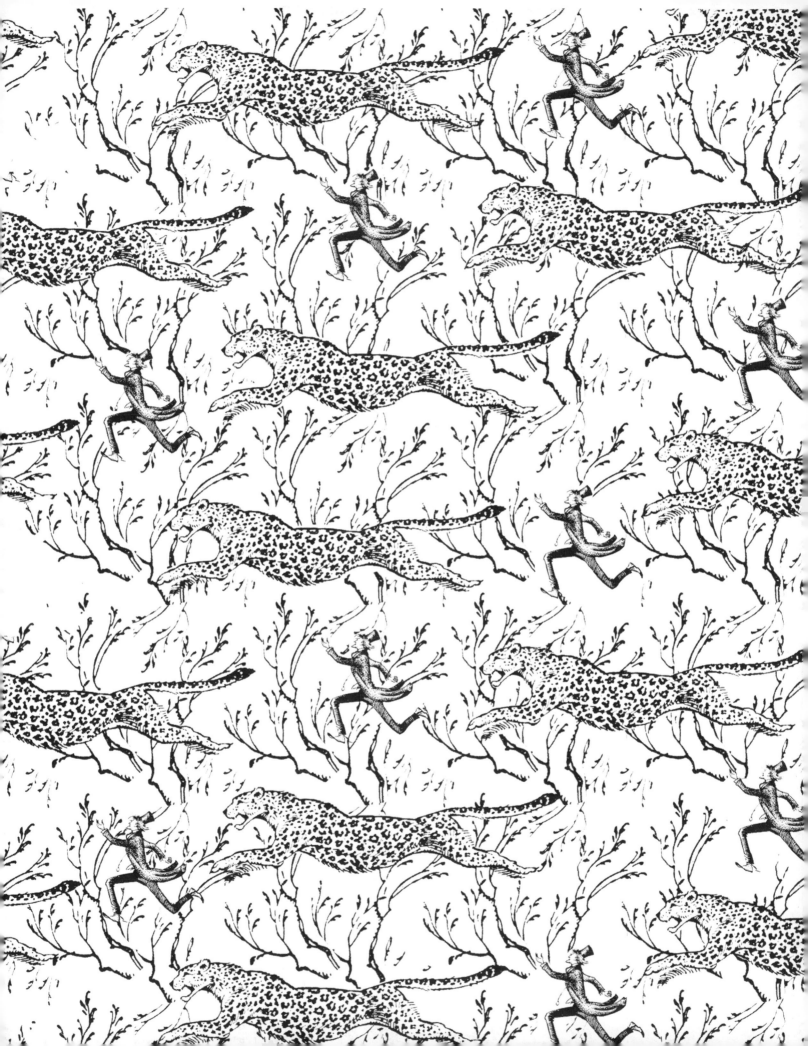

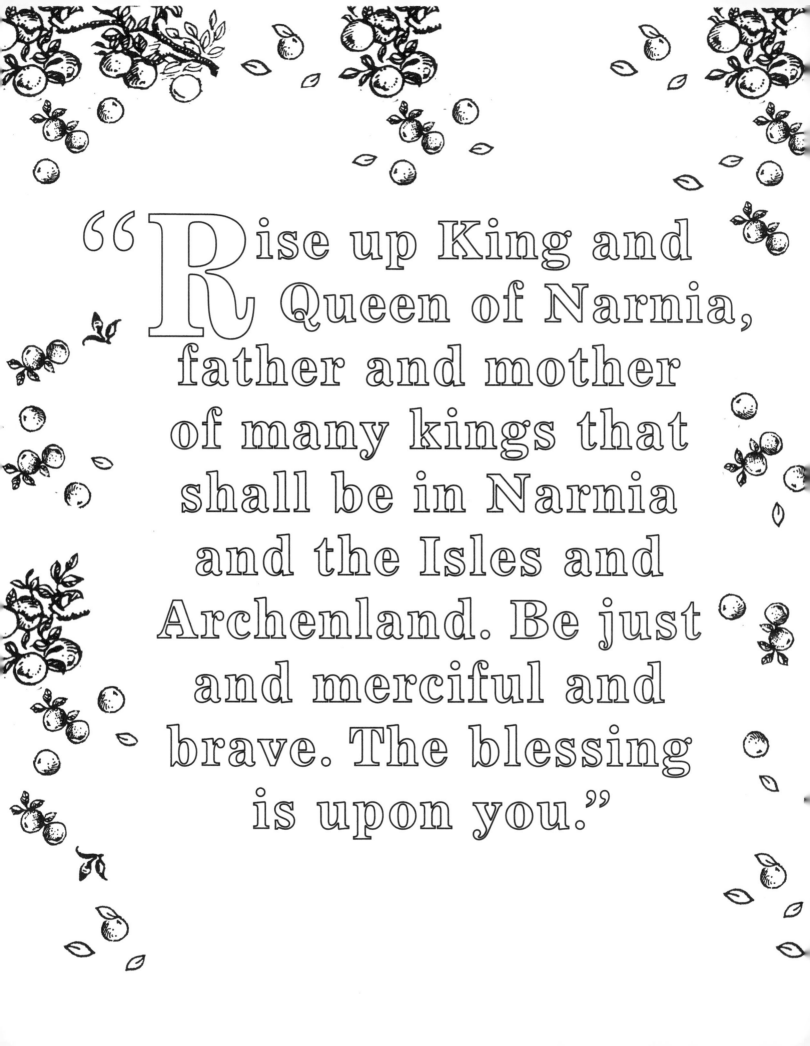

"Rise up King and Queen of Narnia, father and mother of many kings that shall be in Narnia and the Isles and Archenland. Be just and merciful and brave. The blessing is upon you."

THE LION,
THE WITCH AND
THE WARDROBE

SOME DAY BE OLD EN START *Fairy*

—C. S. Lewis

Foreword from THE LION, THE WITCH AND THE WARDROBE

YOU WILL OUGH TO READING *Tales* AGAIN.

Her face was white—
not merely pale, but
white like snow or paper
or icing-sugar, except for
her very red mouth.
It was a beautiful face
in other respects,
but proud and cold
and stern.

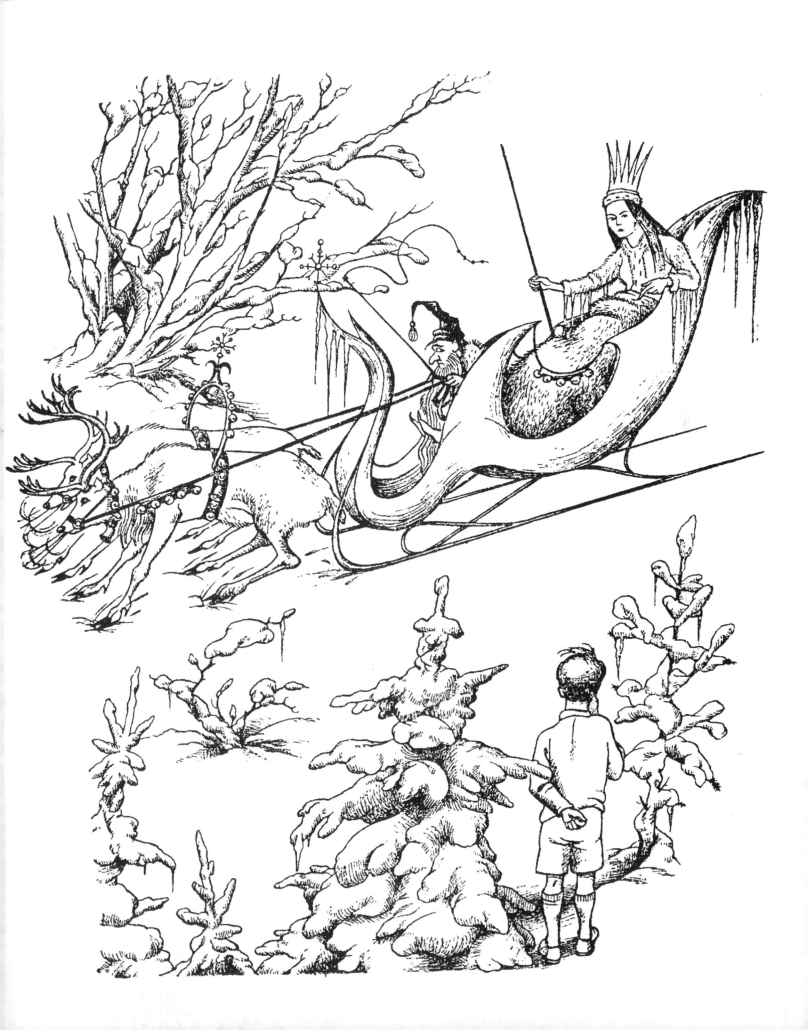

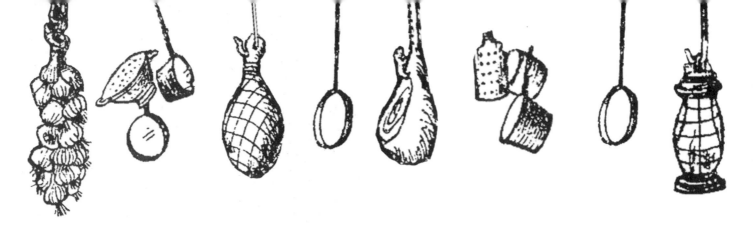

"Aslan?" said Mr. Beaver. "Why, don't you know? He's the King. He's the Lord of the whole wood, but not often here, you understand. Never in my time or my father's time. But the word has reached us that he has come back."

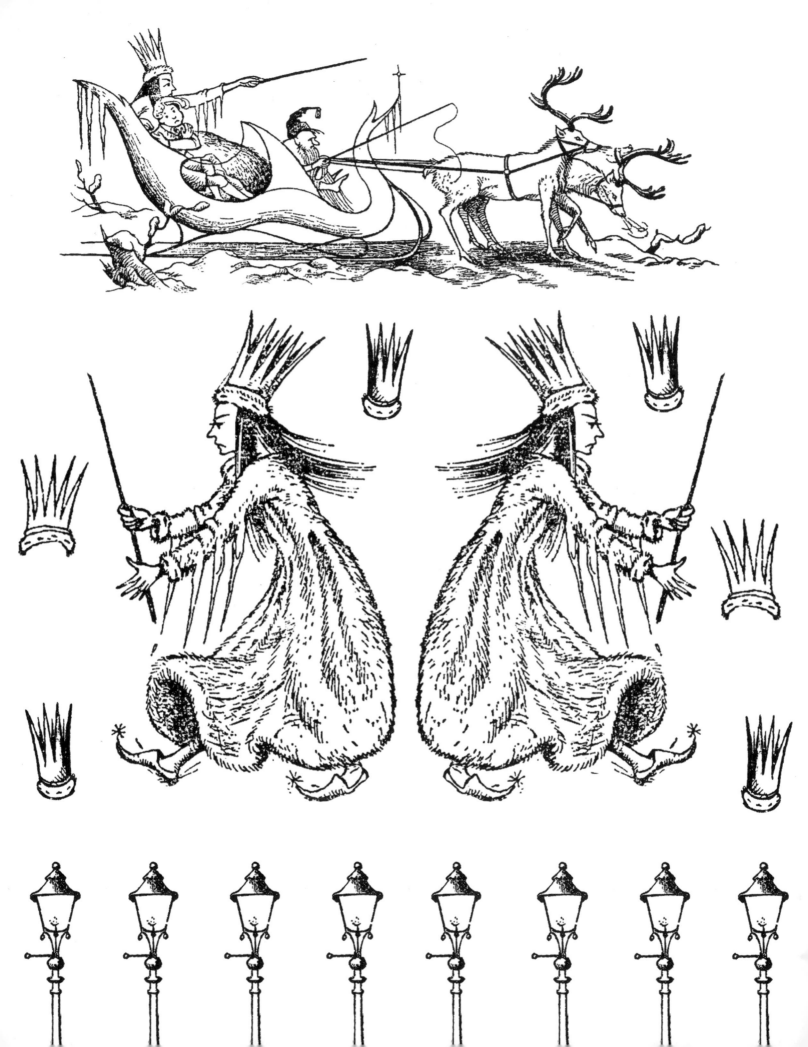

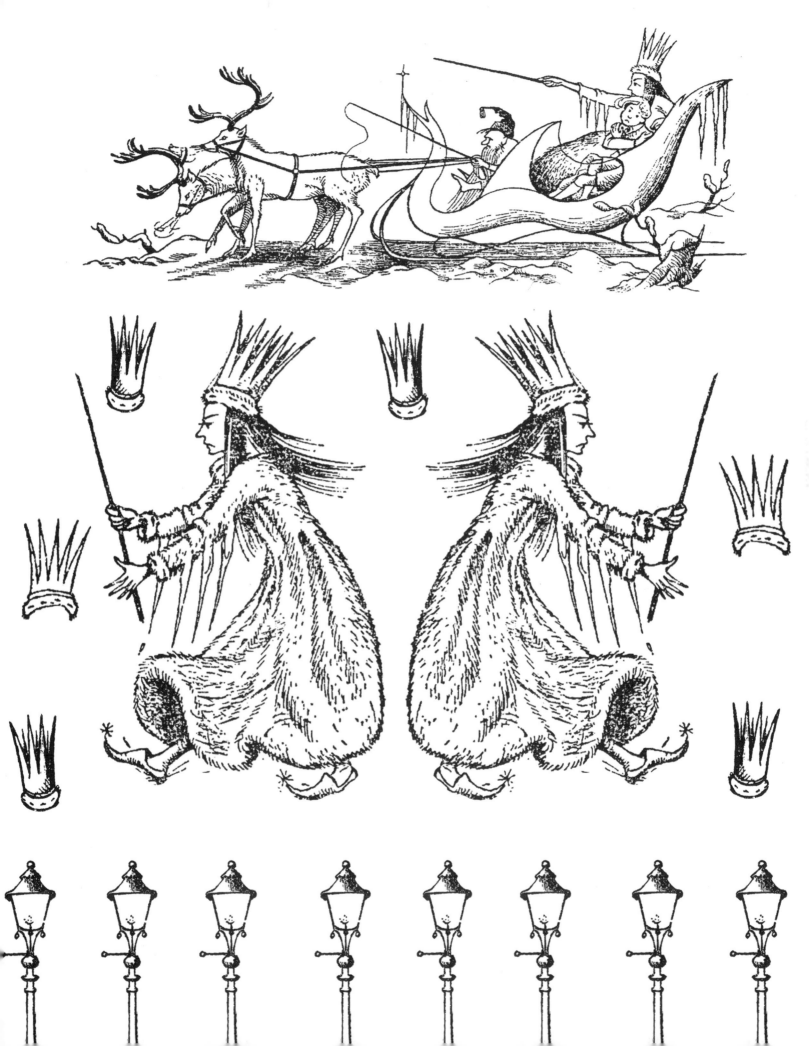

Then with a ROAR from the western shores of the eastern flung himself upon

that shook all Narnia
lamp-post to the
sea the great beast
the WHITE WITCH.

THE HORSE
AND HIS BOY

NOT TO DARE

—Aslan

THE HORSE AND HIS BOY

Mt. Pire

Anvard

pa

narrow gorge

DESERT

Rock

N
W E
S

Stormness Head

to Narnia

ARCHENLAND

R. Winding Arrow

Oasis

DESERT

Tombs   Tashbaan

"I say," said Shasta
in an awed voice.
"This is a wonderful
place!"

"I daresay," said Bree. "But I wish we were safely through it and out at the other side. Narnia and the North!"

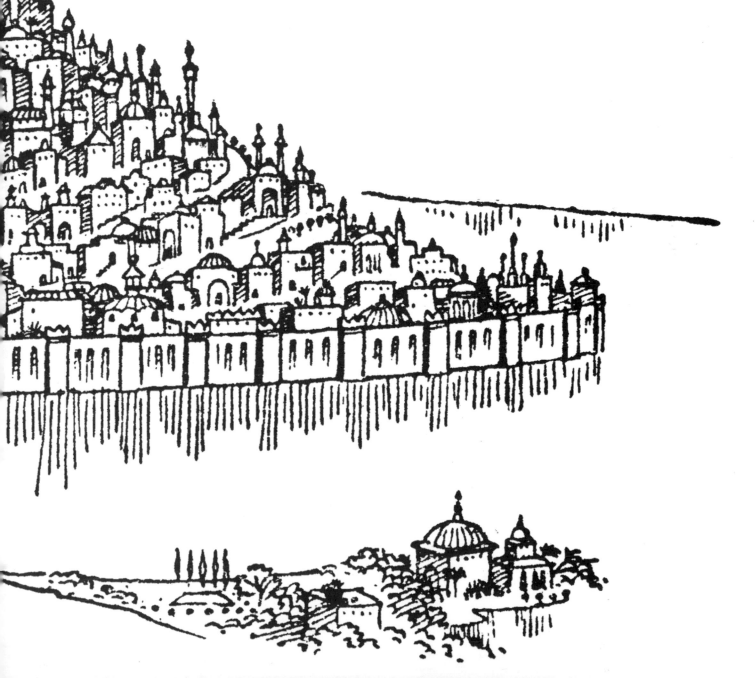

The trumpets sounded again... The noise was coming from the woods to the East, and soon there was a noise of horse-hoofs mixed with it.

A moment later the head of the column came into sight.

PRINCE CASPIAN

I MUST JUST DO IT.

—Lucy

PRINCE CASPIAN

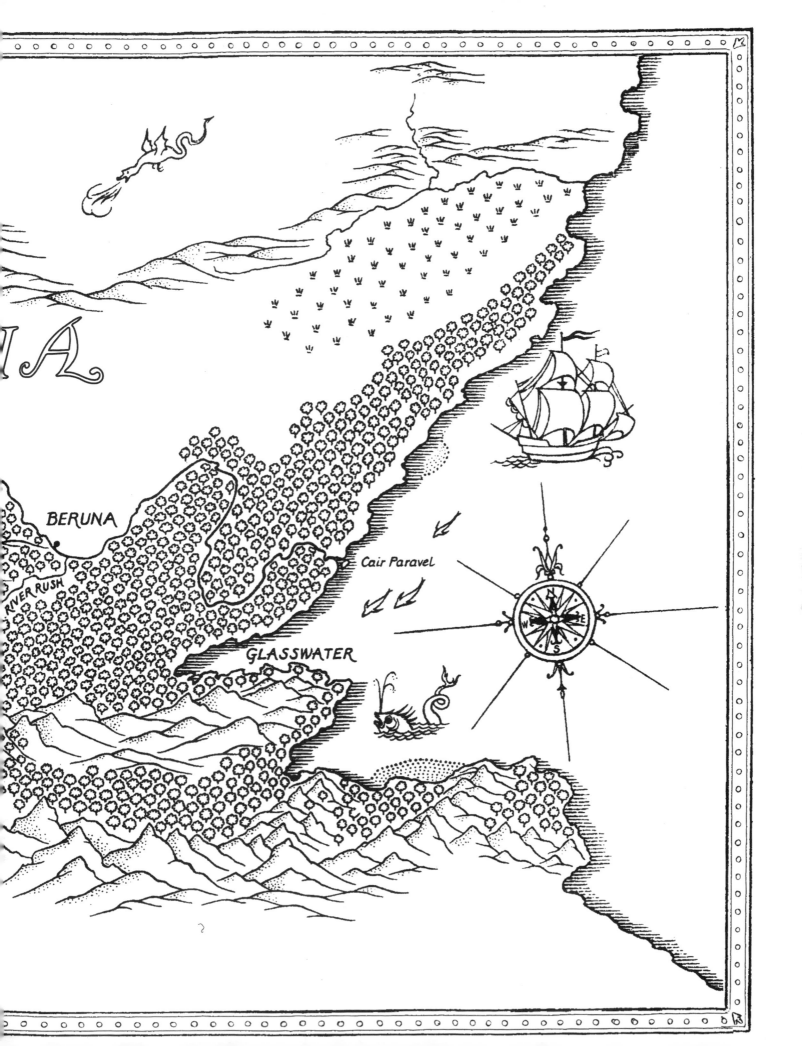

BERUNA

RIVER RUSH

Cair Paravel

GLASSWATER

"**O**–o–o–oh!!" said all the children at once. For now all knew that it was indeed the ancient treasure chamber of Cair Paravel where they had once reigned as Kings and Queens of Narnia.

"**A**slan," said Lucy, "you're bigger."

"That is because you are older, little one," answered he.

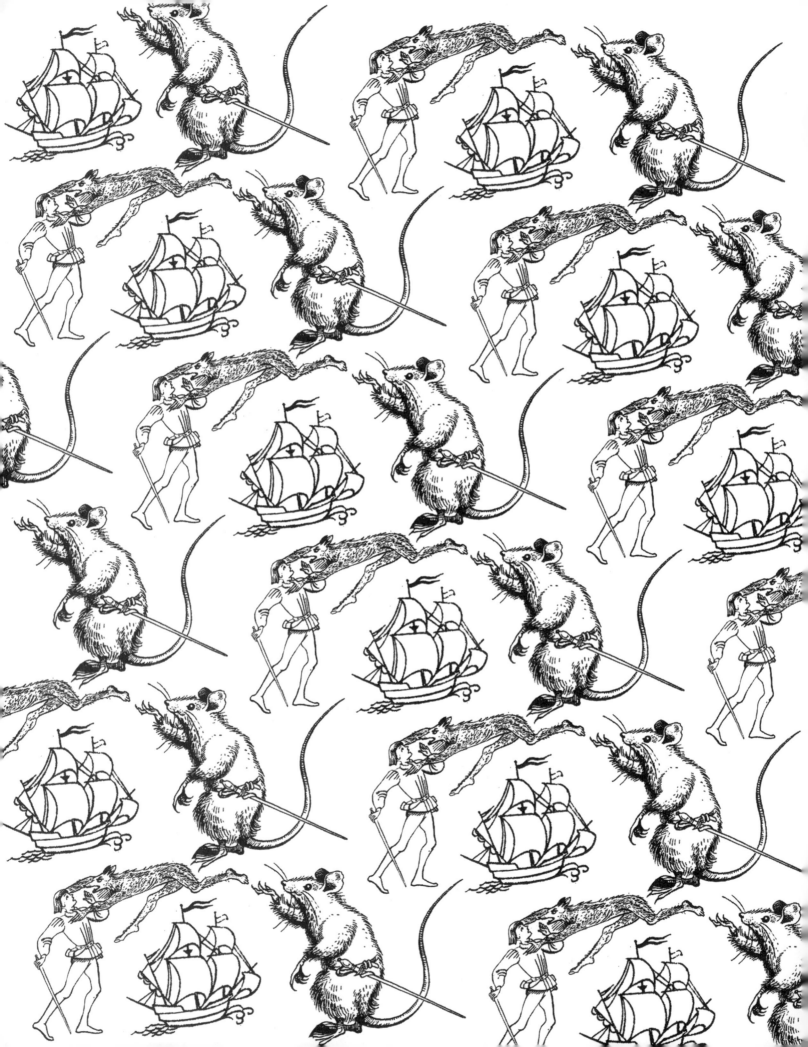

THE VOYAGE OF THE
DAWN TREADER

You can't know. You can only believe

—or not.

About here they joined the ship

The first part of the VOYAGE

FELIMATH THE LONE ISLANDS

DOORN AVRA

THE GREAT EASTERN OCEAN

Now Caspian had begun to teach the Narnians to be sea-faring folk once more, and the *Dawn Treader* was the finest ship he had built yet.

FORECASTLE

lookout man

galley

quarters

starboard

port

Plan of the

Dawn Treader

POOP

tiller

poop deck

hatch

boat

hen coop

Lucy's cabin

Drinian's cabin

stern cabin

Caspian's cabin

As soon as Caspian stepped ashore the crowd broke out into hurrahs and shouts of, "Narnia! Narnia! Long live the King."

THE SILVER CHAIR

You would called to I had been to

not have me unless calling you.

—Aslan

THE SILVER CHAIR

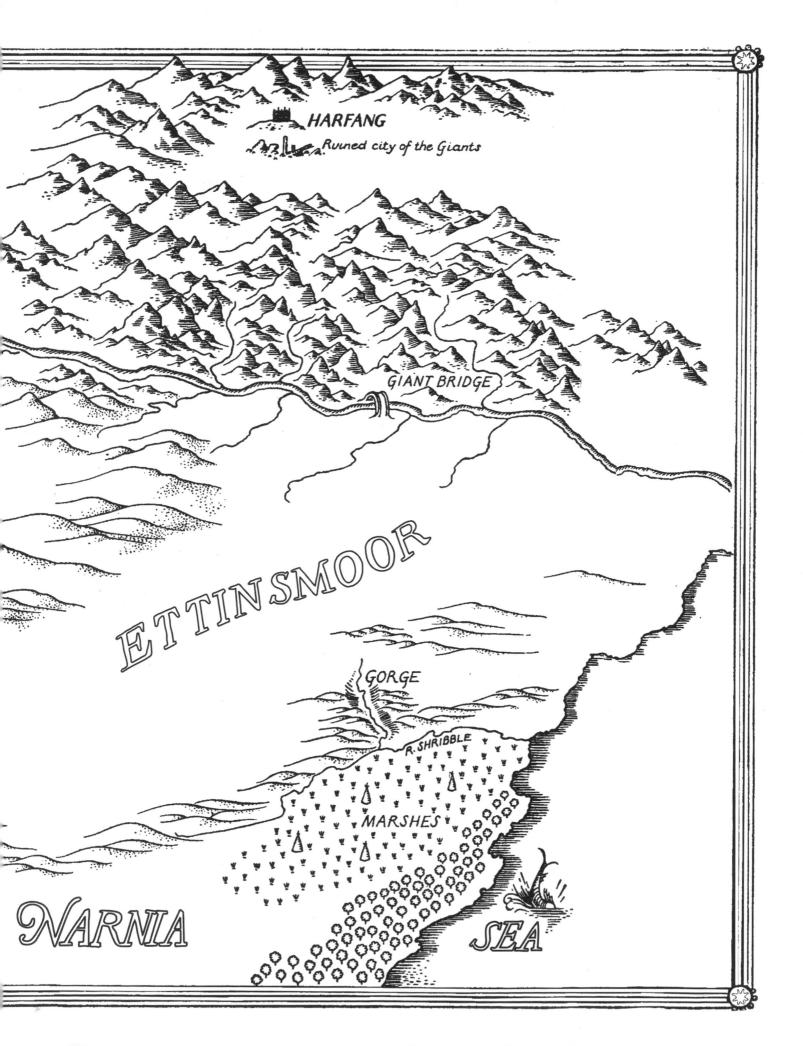

The GIANT

King and Queen looked at each other, nodded to each other, and smiled in a way that Jill didn't exactly like.

"They are all beasts that have found their way down by chasms and caves, out of Overland into the Deep Realm. Many come down, and few return to the sunlit lands. It is said that they will all wake at the end of the world."

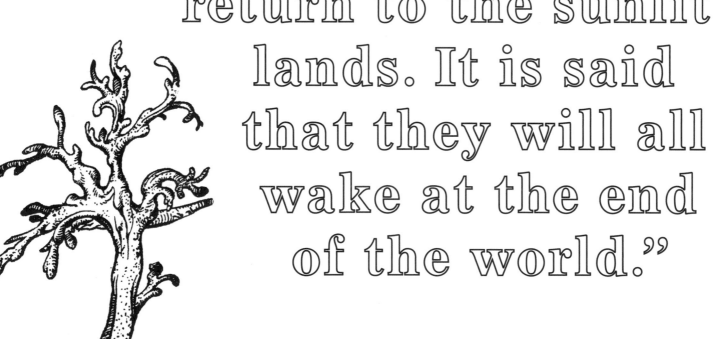

THE LAST BATTLE

—Emeth
THE LAST BATTLE

All find TRULY

what they
SEEK.

"Is Narnia conquered? Has there been a battle?"

"No, Sire," panted the horse, "Aslan is here."

"You see," said Aslan. "They will not let us help them. They have chosen cunning instead of belief. Their prison is only in their own minds...

...But come, children.
I have other work
to do."

And at last, out of the shadow of the trees, racing up the hill for dear life, by thousands and by millions, came all kinds of creatures... And all these ran up to the doorway where Aslan stood.